Animal Colors
Blue Animals

by Christina Leaf

BELLWETHER MEDIA • MINNEAPOLIS, MN

Note to Librarians, Teachers, and Parents:

Blastoff! Readers are carefully developed by literacy experts and combine standards-based content with developmentally appropriate text.

Level 1 provides the most support through repetition of high-frequency words, light text, predictable sentence patterns, and strong visual support.

Level 2 offers early readers a bit more challenge through varied simple sentences, increased text load, and less repetition of high-frequency words.

Level 3 advances early-fluent readers toward fluency through increased text and concept load, less reliance on visuals, longer sentences, and more literary language.

Level 4 builds reading stamina by providing more text per page, increased use of punctuation, greater variation in sentence patterns, and increasingly challenging vocabulary.

Level 5 encourages children to move from "learning to read" to "reading to learn" by providing even more text, varied writing styles, and less familiar topics.

Whichever book is right for your reader, Blastoff! Readers are the perfect books to build confidence and encourage a love of reading that will last a lifetime!

This edition first published in 2019 by Bellwether Media, Inc.

No part of this publication may be reproduced in whole or in part without written permission of the publisher. For information regarding permission, write to Bellwether Media, Inc., Attention: Permissions Department, 6012 Blue Circle Drive, Minnetonka, MN 55343.

Library of Congress Cataloging-in-Publication Data

Names: Leaf, Christina, author.
Title: Blue Animals / by Christina Leaf.
Description: Minneapolis, MN : Bellwether Media, Inc., 2019. | Series:
  Blastoff! Readers. Animal Colors | Audience: Ages 5 to 8. | Audience: K to
  Grade 3. | Includes bibliographical references and index.
Identifiers: LCCN 2018000197 (print) | LCCN 2018005285 (ebook) | ISBN
  9781626178274 (hardcover : alk. paper) | ISBN 9781681035680 (ebook)
Subjects: LCSH: Animals–Color–Juvenile literature. | Blue–Juvenile
  literature.
Classification: LCC QL767 (ebook) | LCC QL767 .L43 2019 (print) | DDC
  591.47/2–dc23
LC record available at https://lccn.loc.gov/2018000197

Editor: Betsy Rathburn   Designer: Jeffrey Kollock

Printed in the United States of America, North Mankato, MN

Table of Contents

Blue Animals

Can you think of many blue animals? It is an uncommon animal color!

regal blue tang

Blue Around You

jeans blueberries sky

Blue whales are the only blue **mammals**. Water **boosts** their blue-gray color.

Flashy Blues

Many animals use blue to show off. Bright bodies help eastern bluebirds find partners.

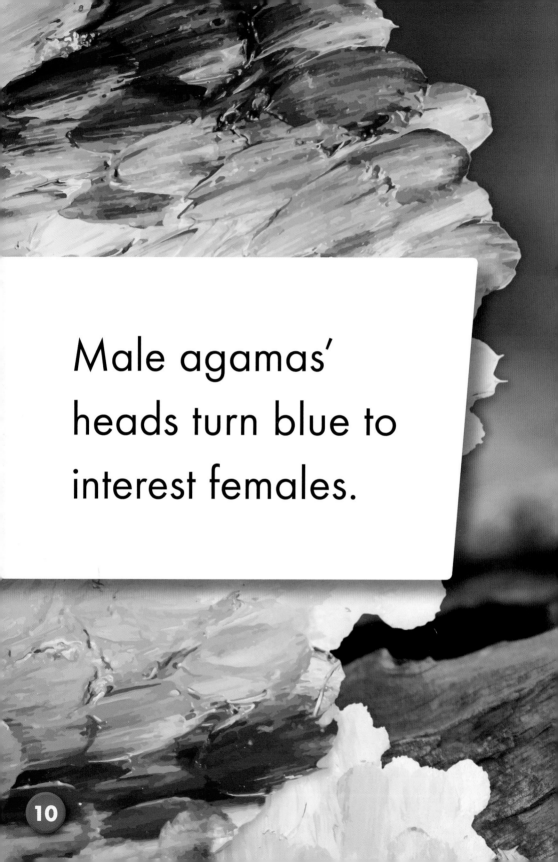

Male agamas' heads turn blue to interest females.

blue-headed
tree agama

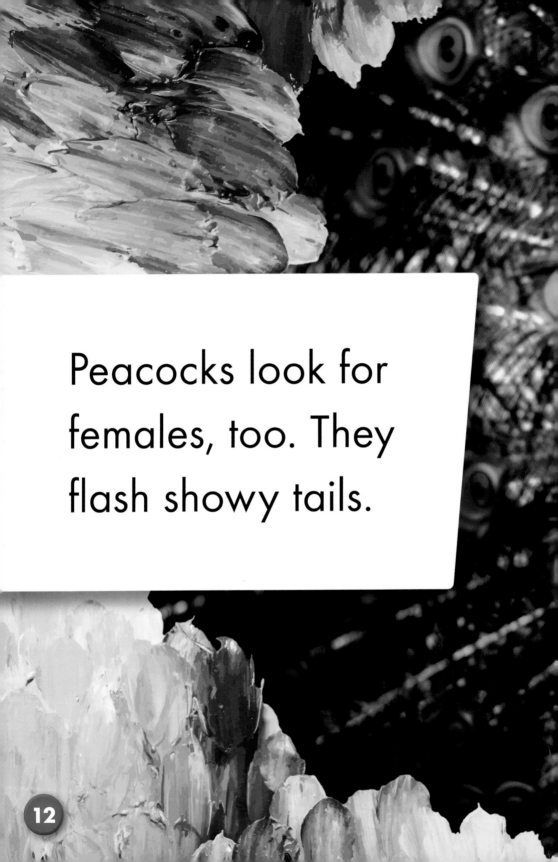

Peacocks look for females, too. They flash showy tails.

Male banded
demoiselles flutter for
females. Blue wing
bands catch the light.

Blue has other uses, too. It **camouflages** blue dragons. They float on the ocean **surface**.

Blue morpho butterflies flash colorful wings as a warning. Stay out of their **territory**!

Some animals are
a mystery. No one
knows why these
tarantulas are blue!

greenbottle
blue tarantula

21

Glossary

boosts

makes something more noticeable

surface

the top or outer part

camouflages

uses color to hide an animal in its surroundings

territory

the home area of an animal

mammals

warm-blooded animals with backbones that feed their young milk

To Learn More

AT THE LIBRARY
Adamson, Heather. *Blue*. Minneapolis, Minn.:
Bullfrog Books, 2014.

Borth, Teddy. *Blue Animals*. Minneapolis, Minn.:
Abdo Kids, 2015.

Hansen, Grace. *Blue Whales*. Minneapolis,
Minn.: Abdo Kids, 2017.

ON THE WEB
Learning more about
blue animals is as easy
as 1, 2, 3.

1. Go to www.factsurfer.com.

2. Enter "blue animals" into the search box.

3. Click the "Surf" button and you will see a list
   of related web sites.

With factsurfer.com, finding more information is
just a click away.

Index